Original title:
Giggling Glades

Copyright © 2025 Creative Arts Management OÜ
All rights reserved.

Author: Dante Kingsley
ISBN HARDBACK: 978-1-80567-252-4
ISBN PAPERBACK: 978-1-80567-551-8

The Amused Archway

Under arching beams, we play,
Laughter echoes in bright array.
Beneath the smiles, the shadows sway,
Tickles of joy, come what may.

Breezes dance with a soft delight,
Turning moments into pure flight.
Secrets shared in the moonlight,
Chasing giggles into the night.

Whirling Dances of Joy

Round and round the laughter spins,
Around the corners, mischief begins.
Feet tap lightly, the world grins,
In the whirl, everyone wins.

Colors flash in a playful chase,
Giggling faces, a cheery embrace.
Every twirl feels like first place,
In this game, we all find grace.

The Mischievous Meadow

In the meadow where daisies hide,
Silly antics we can't abide.
With each peek, the giggles glide,
Nature's whimsy is our guide.

Bouncing flowers share a jest,
Underneath the sun's warm crest.
Whispers of fun, a joyful quest,
In this place, we feel so blessed.

Sprightly Whispers

Through the trees, giggles roam,
Each rustling leaf feels like home.
Shadows chase the light that shone,
In our hearts, we are never alone.

Joyful secrets, light as air,
Sing like birds, without a care.
In this game, we all can share,
Sprightly whispers everywhere.

Sprightly Sunshine

Bubbles pop in golden air,
Sunbeams dance without a care.
Laughter sparkles on the ground,
Joyful whispers all around.

Chasing shadows, bright and quick,
Every giggle a magic trick.
Butterflies in playful flight,
Chasing dreams till day turns night.

Whimsy Among the Leaves

Rustling branches, soft and green,
A secret world, a lively scene.
Squirrels prance with cheeky flair,
Tickling breezes weave through air.

Pinecones tumble, giggles burst,
In this place, fun is a thirst.
Frolicsome critters join the spree,
Nature's laughter, wild and free.

Cheerful Harmony

The brook babbles a merry tune,
 Underneath a smiling moon.
 Daisies sway, a swirly dress,
  In a game of happy mess.

Bouncing beams of daffodil,
 Every moment holds a thrill.
Sunset paints the sky with cheer,
 A chorus of delight draws near.

The Chuckling Forest

Amidst the trees, a raucous jest,
Branches swaying, nature's fest.
Rabbits dash with silly glee,
Caught in fun, they dance so free.

Echoes ring of joyful play,
In this woodsy cabaret.
Frogs and crickets join the choir,
Sparking laughter, never tire.

Lighthearted Trails Through the Thicket

In the woods where shadows play,
Squirrels scamper, bright and gay.
Bubbles float in sunlit air,
Laughter sparkles everywhere.

Rustling leaves, a sudden tease,
Dancing branches sway with ease.
Frogs croak jokes in perfect time,
Nature's giggles in their rhyme.

A rabbit hops with silly flair,
Brightly colored, unaware.
Chasing tails in merry flight,
Joyful hearts in pure delight.

The Merry Dance of Leaf and Sound.

As breezes tickle through the trees,
Whispers float on playful knees.
Petals twirl, a joyful shout,
Nature's chorus all about.

Dandelions spread like cheer,
Swaying gently, bright and near.
Caterpillars, in costume bright,
Join the revel in soft light.

Footsteps echo, heedless prance,
Each tiny creature joins the dance.
With giggles wrapped in leafy sound,
In this haven, joy is found.

Whispers of Laughter

Amidst the woods, a secret hush,
Tiny voices softly brush.
Dancing shadows play their game,
Tickling branches call each name.

Beneath the sky, a canvas bright,
Hiccups of joy take their flight.
Each step brings a cheerful tune,
As chubby clouds embrace the moon.

Mice in hats, a sight to see,
Painting tales from tree to tree.
With laughter echoed all around,
Magic springs from underground.

Secret Meadows of Joy

In fields where giggles never fade,
Dreams are woven, softly laid.
Bouncing blossoms share a grin,
As playful breezes swirl within.

Frolicking fawns join the game,
Each new trick is not the same.
Watch the butterflies flit and twirl,
A dance of joy in dizzy whirl.

Marigolds bloom, painting the ground,
A symphony of joy abounds.
Laughter lingers on the breeze,
In secret meadows, souls find peace.

Whimsy's Embrace

In a meadow bright with cheer,
Laughter echoes, crystal clear.
Breezes dance with a silly sway,
Tickling petals in playful play.

Squirrels prance in a fanciful race,
Chasing shadows, quicken their pace.
Flowers giggle, their colors shout,
In this realm, joy spins about.

Butterflies flit, like jesters bold,
With stories of mischief gently told.
A rabbit grins, with a wink and a hop,
In this embrace, we never stop.

Sunbeams play hide-and-seek with trees,
Filling hearts with lightness and ease.
Here in this realm, laughter's the key,
Unlocking the joy that sets us free.

Dancing with the Daisies

Amidst the blooms, their heads held high,
Daisies twirl beneath the sky.
They sway and bend with glee unbound,
In this dance, pure joy is found.

Frogs leap in a comical line,
Croaking tunes quite out of rhyme.
Their slippery steps are quite a sight,
Under a sunbeam, warm and bright.

Ladybugs giggle, red and round,
As they spin atop the ground.
Each flutter brings a winking cheer,
In fields where laughter draws us near.

With every breeze, the fun ignites,
Creating comedy in the heights.
In playful whispers, secrets tease,
Join the dance, oh, if you please!

Raptures of the Ravine

Down in the dip where the rivers twirl,
The world spins fast, in a joyful whirl.
Rocks chuckle as water splashes,
In this place, time cleverly dashes.

Chirping birds in a chorus sing,
Their silly notes make the heart swing.
Hopping crickets join the fun,
In this jovial race, we all run.

A mischievous breeze steals a hat,
Causing chuckles, imagine that!
With sparkles of sunlight dancing around,
In the ravine, laughter is found.

Each twist and turn an adventure grand,
Where nature unfolds its playful hand.
Here in the rapture, spirits soar,
In the embrace of the land we adore.

The Blissful Boundary

At the edge of dreams where giggles bloom,
A boundary exists that lightens gloom.
Colors collide in a merry hue,
Creating worlds where laughter grew.

Balloons float on a windy tease,
Carrying secrets on the breeze.
Chasing shadows that skip and slide,
In this space, joy takes a ride.

Jesters prance with a wink and a grin,
Inviting all to join in their spin.
While streamers flutter in boundless cheer,
In this boundary, worries disappear.

Hold tight to mirth, let spirits rise,
See the joy in every surprise.
In the blissful confines we will stay,
Dancing through life, come what may!

Joyful Interludes

In the woods where whispers play,
 Laughter floats on a sunny ray.
 Squirrels dance with silly glee,
 Tickling trees, wild and free.

Bouncing bunnies, hops so quick,
 Chasing shadows, a playful trick.
 Frogs in tuxedos leap with grace,
 Drawing giggles, a happy race.

Round and round the flowers spin,
 Each petal holds a cheeky grin.
 Breezes hum a cheerful tune,
 Under the watchful afternoon.

With every step, the joy expands,
 Nature's laughter in joyful bands.
 Here, the smiles come one by one,
 In this place, the fun's never done.

The Laughing Horizon

Where the sun meets the laughing sky,
Children's giggles soar and fly.
Clouds parade in fluffy haste,
Mischief brews; it's a hearty taste.

Puppies tumble, tails a-wag,
Chasing dreams in a boisterous brag.
Jumping puddles, splashes bright,
Every drop is sheer delight.

In the fields, the daisies tease,
Whispering secrets in the breeze.
As butterflies flutter, all around,
Happiness blooms from the ground.

With every chuckle and silly jest,
Nature's belly laughs, it's all the best.
Together we frolic, hoot, and cheer,
For in this moment, joy is here.

Froggy Giggles by the Brook

Frogs in the reeds, they sing with glee,
Jumping and splashing, so wild and free.
With croaks that echo, make quite a sound,
Bringing laughter where joy can be found.

Water bugs dance, a waltz in the sun,
Chasing their shadows, they frolic and run.
The brook bubbles forth, a giggling spree,
Each ripple a chuckle, oh what fun to see!

Nearby the daisies, bees buzz about,
Their tiny, sweet tunes, there's never a doubt.
They tickle the petals, the colors ignite,
Nature's own jesters, a pure delight.

So join in the chorus, let laughter ensue,
In the froggy realm, where joy feels so new.
Amidst all the splendor, we sing and we play,
For who can resist a bright, funny day!

Revelry beneath the Boughs

Under branches wide, the sunlight spills,
Squirrels dash past, all giggles and thrills.
Acorns are flying, a playful treat,
While shadows will dance on the soft, grassy seat.

Chipmunks engage in a lively debate,
Who finds the best snack, oh, what a fate!
In chortles and chuckles, they scurry and soar,
Creating a ruckus, who could ask for more?

With each whispering breeze, the leaves seem to grin,
As laughter erupts from deep down within.
A butterfly flutters, adorned in bright flair,
Joining the revelry, light as the air.

Together we giggle, beneath the green crown,
Every creature a joker, not one wears a frown.
In this merry nook, where hearts intertwine,
The sweetest of moments are simply divine!

The Cheerful Thrum

In the heart of the woods, where the sunlight streams,
The world hums along with whimsical dreams.
A playful parade of bugs on parade,
Their tickling tunes make the best kind of shade.

A dance of the daisies, twirling on high,
Their petals like laughter that reaches the sky.
With whispers of joy on the breezes that blow,
In this vibrant world, smiles always will grow.

The brook gurgles tunes, as it merrily winds,
Through meadows of giggles and curious finds.
Where butterflies flit and birds sing their song,
The playful serenade carries us along.

With each little chuckle, hearts open wide,
In nature's embrace, where we can't help but glide.
In this cheerful thrum, we revel and sway,
Finding glee in each moment, come what may!

Bursting with Merriment

In a glade where laughter hangs thick as the air,
Joy bounces around, a delightful affair.
With echoes of chuckles that dance on the breeze,
Even the tall trees sway, with such perfect ease.

The frogs stage a concert, each note full of glee,
While owls in the branches roll eyes playfully.
The sun bursts through clouds with a twinkle and wink,
In this bubbling habitat, worry won't sink.

Bouncing bright berries, all ripe for the pick,
Merryman creatures delight in the trick.
With every small nibble, a giggle erupts,
As laughter abounds and the fun never stops.

Here, joy flows like rivers, embracing our souls,
With whispers from nature, forever it rolls.
In this merry scene, where smiles overlap,
We're bursting with merriment, wrapped in a map!

Sylvan Serenade

In the woods where shadows dance,
Laughter bubbles, lost in chance.
Squirrels chuckle, rabbits prance,
Joyful moments, nature's romance.

A gentle breeze teases leaves,
Whispering secrets, playful thieves.
Sunlight flickers, shadows weave,
Giggles echo, hearts believe.

Among the trees, a starlit show,
Dancing fireflies, a twinkling glow.
Summer nights, with magic flow,
Nature's joy, a sprightly flow.

In every nook, sweet echoes ring,
Mischief blooms, what joy they bring.
With every rustle, whispers sing,
In this forest, we all swing.

Echoes of Playful Light

Beneath the canopy, giggles rise,
Jumping shadows chase the skies.
Bubbles burst, and laughter flies,
Nature's charm, a sweet surprise.

The brook babbles with playful cheer,
Winding whispers fill the ear.
Frogs leap high, with none to fear,
In this realm, all is dear.

Sunbeams filtered, beams so bright,
Tickling flowers, oh what a sight!
Chasing clouds in sheer delight,
A symphony of joy and light.

With every step, fun we create,
Wandering paths, we celebrate.
In this land, where we relate,
Laughter echoes; it's never late.

Meadow Mischief

In the meadow, games unfold,
Secrets whispered, tales retold.
Bouncing daisies, brave and bold,
Nature's laughter, purest gold.

A butterfly flits, a cheeky tease,
Daring us to glide with ease.
Each moment holds a sweet reprise,
In this haven of endless pleas.

Rolling hills, we tumble down,
Joy ignited, never a frown.
With each giggle, a legacy's crown,
In this laughter, we all drown.

Humming tunes the crickets play,
In tune with nature, come what may.
Mischief dances through the day,
Sprightly spirits lead the way.

Frisky Breezes

Whirling winds through branches glide,
With each gust, let laughter ride.
Bursts of joy on every side,
In this realm, we take in stride.

Petals swirl in breezy flight,
Tickling cheeks in pure delight.
Through the glens, what a sight!
Nature's pranks, both day and night.

A playful tune the robins sing,
Chirpy notes like springtime's fling.
With every call, our hearts take wing,
In this escapade, we all swing.

From sunlit meadows to shaded woods,
Every corner, mischief broods.
Together here, all moods include,
Boundless laughter, our hearts elude.

Flickering Smiles

In a meadow where shadows dance,
Each flower sways in merry chance.
The sunbeams tug, a playful tease,
While laughter whispers through the trees.

Breezes tickle, gentle and light,
Colorful sprites, out of sight.
They paint the air with giggles bright,
In this realm, joy takes its flight.

With every step, a merry sound,
Tiny critters leap around.
Joyful echoes fill the air,
A world of wonder, free from care.

When night comes in, the moon will grin,
With twinkling stars, the fun begins.
In every nook, a friendly face,
In this quaint, enchanted place.

Fanciful Footprints

Along the path where shadows grow,
Each step a spark, a bubble's flow.
Tiny toes leave marks in sand,
A map of joy by nature's hand.

Bouncing blooms with colors wild,
Invite the laughter of each child.
The giggles glide on softest wings,
As nature hums and sweetly sings.

Pixies twirl in a playful spree,
While rabbits hop, oh so carefree.
Every footprint, a hint of glee,
As joy unfolds, where hearts agree.

A whimsy dance in morning light,
A world alive, a pure delight.
In every turn, a surprise awaits,
With fanciful paths, the joy creates.

Merry Echoes of Nature

In the hush of leafy boughs,
Nature giggles, but not quite how.
A rustling leaf, a playful shout,
With every sound, joy jumps about.

Hopping frogs in splashes bright,
Chase the beams of flickering light.
Bouncing bees in jolly flight,
Bring melodious laughter light.

Over hills, the echoes ring,
With each chirp, the woodlands sing.
A chorus of merry delight,
In every nook, by day and night.

As dusk descends, hilarity grows,
In shadowed corners, whimsy flows.
Nature's voice, a sweet refrain,
Wraps the world in laughter's chain.

The Jubilant Journey

On winding trails where giggles thrive,
The spirit dances, hearts alive.
Every step, a joyful cheer,
With bouncing moods that draw you near.

Bright sunsets paint the evening sky,
While playful breezes flutter by.
In every twirl, a thrill unfolds,
As laughter's warmth the sunset holds.

Through meadows bright and valleys deep,
The merry song invites a leap.
With each twist, the fun expands,
A jubilant journey hand in hand.

At every crossroad, blissful sights,
Unruly sounds and fancy flights.
Adventure calls—come take your chance,
In laughter's glow, let spirits dance.

Whispers of the Joyful Forest

In the woods where shadows dance,
Squirrels plot a merry chance.
With acorns tossed and giggles bright,
The trees sway in pure delight.

Frogs wear crowns of lily pads,
Dancing in their leafy fads.
Breezes tease the branches low,
Tickling leaves that sway to and fro.

Amid the ferns, a rabbit peeks,
With a grin that slyly sneaks.
Playing hide and seek with ease,
In the laughter of the trees.

Giggling streams run swift and fast,
Whispers of both present and past.
Nature joins the playful spree,
In the heart of revelry.

Laughter Amongst the Moss

Beneath the boughs, the soft ground sighs,
   As hidden critters share their whys.
  Mossy beds where giggles bloom,
   Nature's laughter fills the room.

Toadstools wear their polka dots,
In this realm where joy connects the spots.
The sunlight sprinkles, warm and bright,
   Each glimmer adds to pure delight.

A squirrel spins in wild pirouettes,
  While chipmunks scatter, no regrets.
With each jump, a sound so sweet,
   It's a grand parade on tiny feet.

Whispers float in a playful tune,
  Underneath the watchful moon.
In these woods, the fun won't cease,
  Here, in nature, joy finds peace.

The Secret Meadow's Chuckle

In a meadow, secrets play,
Where daisies nod throughout the day.
Butterflies dance in the sun's warm gaze,
Chasing laughter through the maze.

Bumblebees hum a joyful song,
As flowers sway, the breeze is strong.
Each petal sings, a soft delight,
Painting colors, pure and bright.

Gentle whispers by the brook,
In every nook, a giggling look.
With every splash, the joy is found,
In this realm, where hearts abound.

A laughter bubble fills the air,
In this land without a care.
Every creature, great and small,
Shares a chuckle, one and all.

Echoes of Playful Breezes

In the air, a giggle swirls,
Tickling branches, as laughter twirls.
Whispers ride on winds so light,
Carrying joy, both day and night.

Leaves converse in softest tones,
While shadows dance on ancient stones.
Every flicker, every leap,
Holds a secret, oh so deep.

Clouds drift by with cheerful glee,
As sunbeams play hide and seek with me.
Nature's pulse, a playful tease,
Brings a smile with every breeze.

From hilltops high to valleys low,
The echoes of laughter flow.
In this realm of fun and cheer,
Joyous whispers bring us near.

Riddles in the Woods

In the shade where shadows play,
A squirrel jokes, runs away.
Trees whisper secrets, woven tight,
Echoes of laughter in the light.

A rabbit hops, a trickster's cheer,
With winks and grins, it draws us near.
Mushrooms chuckle, underfoot,
In a maze of giggles, we pursue.

The owl twirls, up in the flight,
With wise old hoots, a funny sight.
Nature's jesters, all around,
In this wild place, joy is found.

So come and dance among the trees,
Join in the riddle, feel the breeze.
In this realm of mirth and play,
We'll laugh the sunset into day.

Playful Petals Dance

Petals spin on breezy days,
Twirling in the sunlit rays.
Colors burst, a vivid show,
In this garden, giggles flow.

The daisies hide with cheeky glee,
As butterflies tease and flutter free.
Honeybees hum a silly tune,
Join the blooms by afternoon.

A gentle breeze begins to tease,
Caressing stems, swaying leaves.
Nature's laughter, bright and clear,
Calls out to all who venture near.

With every rustle, every sway,
The hilarity is here to stay.
In petals' dance, we find delight,
A playful world, out of sight.

Swaying with Laughter

Beneath the sun, the branches sway,
In the forest, fun holds sway.
Laughter rings, a merry sound,
In this funny patch of ground.

The creek chuckles, bubbling clear,
Tickling toes who venture near.
A friendly breeze with mischief in store,
Tickles your neck and sends you to the floor.

The ferns shimmy, the flowers spin,
In a dance where giggles begin.
Squirrels scurry, hiding snacks,
In this playful woodland pact.

So join the fun, sway side to side,
Let laughter be your joyful guide.
In this haven, wild and free,
We'll sway with glee, just you and me.

The Breezy Laughing Paths

On winding ways where breezes tease,
    Giggles float upon the leaves.
The sunbeams slide from tree to tree,
    Leading the way with glee.

Each step we take, a chuckle blooms,
    As nature plays in playful tunes.
The pebbles giggle, soft and sly,
    Underfoot, they laugh and lie.

The path ahead, a jolly jest,
Around each corner, joy is blessed.
The whispering willows share a smile,
    Inviting laughter for a while.

So wander down these paths of cheer,
    With every footfall, joy draws near.
    In this landscape, light and bright,
We stroll through laughter, pure delight.

Sunlit Clearing of Laughter

In the bright patch of sun, they play,
With giggles that chase clouds away.
Laughter echoes, light as a song,
Winding through trees where they belong.

Bubbles float, shimmer in the rays,
Children leap in joyful displays.
Fluffy critters join in the fun,
Chasing shadows, sprinting to run.

Dancing Shadows in the Thicket

Witty whispers flit between the trees,
While playful breezes stir the leaves.
Swirls of laughter weave like a thread,
Where even the flowers raise their head.

Puppies twirl, tails wagging fast,
In a world where worries don't last.
Every rustle holds a cheeky sound,
Echoing joy that knows no bounds.

Chuckles in the Sunbeams

Sunbeams spark like twinkling eyes,
As funny fables begin to rise.
Bouncing bunnies trade silly jokes,
While the playful sun tickles the folks.

Chasing shadows, a frolicsome race,
In this sunlit, enchanted space.
Every heart dances, every spirit lifts,
Amidst the giggles and playful drifts.

The Enchanted Grove's Delight

Whimsy whispers through the trees,
Funny antics carried by the breeze.
Fairies giggle, winking with glee,
Spreading cheer with a sprightly spree.

With each rustle, a secret shared,
In the grove where laughter has fared.
Beneath the boughs, joy intertwines,
Life's silly moments in perfect designs.

The Quirky Quagmire

In a muddy patch where ducks do dance,
Twirling and flapping, they take a chance.
With wobbly steps and feathers so bright,
They leap and plop with pure delight.

A squirrel nearby, with acorns in tow,
Tries to join in but slips in the flow.
Rolling and tumbling, what a great sight,
Laughter erupts, oh what a night!

The frogs start to croak, a silly tune,
Under the glow of a cheeky moon.
Jumping around in their joyful spree,
Creating a ruckus, oh so carefree.

With friends all around, it's a merry throng,
Where silliness reigns and everyone's strong.
In this quirky patch, where joy is a game,
Every giggle shared, adds to the fame.

Gleeful Glimmers

Amidst the flowers that twist and twirl,
Bumblebees buzz in a happy whirl.
Petals are bobbing in playful flight,
A peacock struts, such a colorful sight.

The sunbeams dance on the sparkling brook,
While a cat with a hat writes a silly book.
Tap-tap-tapping on the windowpane,
Raindrops join in, singing with the rain.

A rabbit hops past, wearing shoes of green,
With a twinkle of joy, it's quite the scene.
Chasing after butterflies, oh what a chase,
In these gleeful glimmers, we find our place.

Laughter erupts with every surprise,
As silly antics fill the skies.
In a world where smiles bloom and grow,
Fun is the language, this we all know.

The Cheery Nook

In a cozy corner where the sun shines bright,
Chairs spin around in a whimsical flight.
With cushions that giggle and tickle the toes,
Every corner whispers where laughter flows.

A parrot tells jokes, with a squawk and a grin,
While a cat tells stories of mischief and sin.
A tea party blossoms with cakes piled high,
Sipping on laughter, oh my, oh my!

The gnomes in the garden with hats full of cheer,
Dance with the daisies, bring all the fun near.
They tickle each other and leap with glee,
In this cheery nook, everyone's free.

In the middle of play, with hearts full of light,
Every day here feels utterly right.
Sharing sweet moments, joy not forsook,
Life flows like honey in this cheery nook.

Frolicsome Fantasies

In a land where giggles paint the skies,
Frogs wear crowns, much to our surprise!
Turtles race on roller skates, so bold,
Each twist and turn brings laughter untold.

A jack-in-the-box pops with an glee,
Jumping out, shouting, "Come play with me!"
Balloons filled with giggles float through the air,
Creating a spectacle beyond compare.

In this fanciful place, every dream springs,
Silly kangaroos sport musical bling.
With every hop, they hum a sweet song,
In frolicsome fantasies where all belong.

Every twist of fate and silly despair,
Turns into joy as we float on air.
Together we weave tales that won't fade,
In this land of fun, where joy's remade.

Frolicking Foliage

In the shade where whispers play,
Leaves dance lightly, come what may.
Squirrels chase their tails with glee,
Nature's jesters, wild and free.

Breezes tickle branches tall,
Laughter echoes, a beckoning call.
Flowers wink in vibrant hues,
As petals share their secret muse.

Underneath the dappled light,
Creatures frolic, pure delight.
Ants march in a silly line,
Each step a giggle, oh so fine.

In this realm where joy resides,
Every shadow, a fun surprise.
With each rustle, chuckles rise,
In nature's arms, laughter flies.

Mirth in the Greenwood

Beneath the trees, a giggle stirs,
As playful winds tease budding furs.
Chirping crickets sing along,
A merry tune, lively and strong.

Bouncing bunnies jump and spin,
Chasing tails of furry kin.
Bright sunbeams catch a skipping fox,
Every leap, a box of socks!

The bubbling brook hums a jest,
Splashing water, a jolly quest.
Mirthful mushrooms peek and grin,
In this enclave, laughter's kin.

With each whisper of the night,
Stars join in, a twinkling sight.
In the greenwood, joy concedes,
A world of fun that never pleads.

The Jolly Saplings

Young trees sway with giddy cheer,
Branches bend, no hint of fear.
They play tag with the passing breeze,
Rustling softly, the world to tease.

Buds burst forth in curious ways,
Drawing smiles with their leafy displays.
Each frond a giggle, light and spry,
In this forest, laughter's nigh.

Wobbly deer prance here and there,
Sharing jokes without a care.
Even shadows join the fun,
All creatures revel, every one.

As dusk descends with stars aglow,
Whispers of joy in moonlight flow.
In this haven, bliss remains,
Jolly saplings are the gains.

Delighted Footsteps

Pitter-patter on the ground,
Every step, a joyful sound.
Butterflies with giggles flit,
In this dance, they never quit.

Laughter bubbles from the stream,
Rippling waters share a dream.
Dandelions join the race,
As fingers tickle nature's face.

Hopping frogs in playful jest,
Lily pads, their cozy nest.
With each leap, a splash and squeal,
Nature's laughter, pure and real.

In sunshine's glow and twilight's hum,
Delighted footsteps fill with fun.
Every corner holds a cheer,
In this world where smiles appear.

Echoes of Laughter in the Wind

In a place where shadows play,
Laughter dances, bright and gay.
Whispers tease the sleepy trees,
Joyful echoes ride the breeze.

Squirrels chatter, chasing dreams,
Sunlight sparkles, glinting beams.
A ticklish breeze spins tales anew,
As giggles swirl in shades of blue.

Jolly critters prance around,
Painting smiles upon the ground.
Wondrous moments spun with glee,
In this realm of jubilee.

With every hop and playful cheer,
The atmosphere is bright and clear.
In this place, joy takes a spin,
Where laughter flutters, let's begin!

Joyful Spirits Beneath the Boughs

Amidst the leaves, where shadows play,
Joyful spirits frolic all day.
Beneath the boughs, a playful spree,
Every chuckle feels so free.

The pond reflects a dancing glee,
As dragonflies hum in harmony.
Furry friends in joyful chase,
Brighten up this merry place.

When dandelions twirl and sway,
They whisper secrets of the day.
With each gust, the giggles soar,
In playful joy, who could ask for more?

With laughter ringing through the air,
All worries seem to disappear.
In this haven, life is grand,
Where funny antics fill the land.

Frolics and Frivolities of the Foliage

Under the canopy, fun unfolds,
With frolics bright, and secrets told.
Leaves jiggle in a merry dance,
Inviting all to take a chance.

The sunbeams play, they skip and hop,
On dancing petals, they never stop.
A chorus of chirps joins the cheer,
As happiness draws ever near.

Crickets strum their nightly tune,
While fireflies twinkle like stars at noon.
Every rustle, a giggle shared,
In this enchanted realm, none are scared.

With chuckles bright, and hearts aglow,
Joy ricochets, where laughter flows.
In this sanctuary where fun resides,
Life's whimsical rhythm happily abides.

Enchanted Trills of the Meadow

In electric whispers through the grass,
The meadow sings as moments pass.
With each trill and fluttering sound,
Joyful surprises are easily found.

Around the blooms, where smiles sprout,
Happy antics spin about.
Every hum, a tune of cheer,
Inviting laughter, drawing near.

The breeze tickles, the daisies grin,
A humorous twist in the merry din.
Chasing shadows, we skip and play,
With radiant spirits, we seize the day.

In this mirthful, whimsical glen,
Life bursts forth again and again.
Here, in playful harmony,
Laughter reigns, wild and free.

Whimsy Amongst the Wildflowers

In fields where colors twist and play,
The blooms are laughing, bright and gay.
A bee on roller skates whirls by,
Tickling the petals, oh my, oh my!

The daisies dance a wobbly tune,
While butterflies leap like balloons.
A ladybug dons a tiny hat,
And the grasshoppers leap to chat.

With every breeze, a chuckle swells,
As nature's secret giggle dwells.
Swaying blooms in a playful show,
Invite all creatures to join the flow.

In this enchanted, silly scene,
Life's little quirks reign supreme.
Hearts grown light in the sunlit hour,
In the whispers of each vibrant flower.

Serenade of the Swaying Grasses

When gentle winds begin to tease,
The grasses sway like giggling bees.
Beneath their dance, a secret song,
Of laughter where both hearts belong.

The tall blades bow, then rise with cheer,
A gentle sway, a whisper here.
In every dip, a funny quirk,
Where even shadows seem to smirk.

Small critters join the merry play,
In hops and skips throughout the day.
The sunbeams wink down from the blue,
As nature laughs, and so do you.

So close your eyes and feel the breeze,
Let's join the fun beneath the trees.
In this joyful, swaying art,
The funny side ignites the heart.

Chuckling Streams and Beaming Skies

A stream skips stones with a giggly splash,
As sunlight dances in a dandy flash.
Fish in the water play peek-a-boo,
While frogs declare, "Come join us too!"

Clouds float by in a cotton candy race,
Each one has a smile upon its face.
Raindrops twirl like little bells,
Dancing on leaves, where laughter dwells.

The sunbeams tickle the flowers bright,
While the world embraces sheer delight.
In this merry scene, joy takes flight,
As skies and streams share laughter's light.

So dip your feet and join the fun,
With each giggle, day's work is done.
Nature's chorus fills the air,
Where every moment's without a care.

The Elves' Delightful Revelry

Beneath the moon, the elves all peek,
With tiny hats and shoes so chic.
They twirl and leap in joyous glee,
Creating mischief by the tree.

In moonlit meadows, laughter's spread,
With funny tales and dreams ahead.
They tickle toadstools, share a wink,
And dance along the merry brink.

Fireflies flash like silly stars,
Guiding the elves in their sweet cars.
A game of hide and seek begins,
With fits of laughter, carefree spins.

So join the night where magic's found,
In every giggle, joy abounds.
These merry elves will lead the way,
In the heart of night where dreams shall sway.

Chortling Canopies

Beneath the leaves so green, they sway,
Laughter echoes, come what may.
Squirrels dance on branches high,
Twisting, turning, oh my my!

A rabbit hops with comic flair,
Wiggling ears, without a care.
The breeze joins in, a giggling breeze,
Whispers secrets through the trees.

Sunbeams flicker, a playful tease,
Casting shadows that bend and please.
Nature's jest, in every sound,
Joyful antics all around.

The world a stage, so bright and bold,
Every whisper a story told.
So come, dear friends, let's dance and play,
In this merry land, we'll stay.

The Jester's Grove

In a realm where laughter plays,
Jesters weave their funny ways.
With every step, the flowers sway,
Tickling thoughts that jump and play.

A crow caws out a silly rhyme,
Echoing through the trees in clime.
A fox prances, shoes of lace,
In this forest, joy finds grace.

Butterflies wear a wink and grin,
Swirling colors, let fun begin.
Beneath the arch of sunlit trees,
Fun is found in every breeze.

So gather 'round, put worries away,
Join the jest in nature's play.
In this grove where chuckles bloom,
Laughter dances, void of gloom.

Sunlit Frolics

The dappled light, a quilt of cheer,
Where giggles jump from ear to ear.
A playful breeze flits through the grass,
Shadows leap and moments pass.

Daisies nod in rhythm sweet,
As children whirl on nimble feet.
The sun above, a laughing friend,
Inviting joy that has no end.

A pond nearby, a wink of blue,
Where frogs jump high, with jokes anew.
With splashes loud and giggles bright,
Playtime rules in this delight.

So let your heart be merry, light,
In sun-kissed glades, our spirits flight.
Together here, we laugh and spin,
In frolics warm, let life begin.

The Blooming Lightheartedness

Colorful blooms in a lively dance,
Whisking feelings, a bright romance.
With petals soft and scents so sweet,
Every turn, a funny feat.

The bees are buzzing, full of glee,
Chasing dreams from flower to tree.
A butterfly flutters, a clown in flight,
Spreading laughter, pure delight.

With giggles sprinkled on the morn,
From every bud, a prank is born.
Joyful whispers in the air,
A symphony of playful care.

So roam these paths, embrace the cheer,
Where happiness flows, crystal clear.
In blooms so bright, let spirits rise,
Under the vast and joyful skies.

Bliss in the Thicket

In playful woods where shadows dance,
The critters prance, they take a chance.
A squirrel twirls with acorn bold,
While giggles spill like tales retold.

Beneath the trees, a stream will sing,
As frogs in crowns leap with a swing.
The bumblebees buzz tunes so sweet,
Where laughter's echo finds its beat.

A bunny hops, with wiggle and twist,
Chasing sunbeams, none can resist.
With every rustle, joy ignites,
In the thicket where mirth invites.

So if you wander these woods so fine,
Expect to find a silly line.
With every smile, the world aligns,
In blissful moments, joy entwines.

Laughter's Hidden Retreat

Behind the hills, where secrets play,
A nook of giggles, bright and gay.
The flowers bloom in cheeky hues,
With whispers soft, they tease and muse.

A jester's hat on every sprout,
With petals curled, they dance about.
The sun dips low, a golden grin,
As nature's joke begins to spin.

Watch rabbits wear their silly socks,
And turtles race, the clock mocks!
A riddle shared beneath the sky,
As clouds above just drift on by.

In this retreat, where laughter brews,
The world is painted in joyful views.
Let every moment tickle your heart,
For in this space, we play our part.

Radiant Rows of Delight

In rows of colors, laughter blooms,
Amidst the light, where joy resumes.
The daisies nod, with cheeky flair,
While butterflies flit without a care.

A skipping frog in polka dots,
A curious fox ties up the knots.
With wagging tails and playful prance,
The sunbeams join in this merry dance.

The breeze brings giggles, soft and clear,
As nature whispers, 'Come, draw near!'
With every sway, the ground will shake,
For moments shared are laughs we make.

In radiant rows, such joy ignites,
With every glance, our heart takes flight.
So linger here, let laughter show,
In fields of smiles, let good times grow.

Lighthearted Reverie

In dreams of whimsy, we take our flight,
Where rosy clouds drift in pure delight.
A jolly tune floats on the breeze,
While giggles dance among the trees.

With curious eyes, the owls confide,
In tales of folly, they take great pride.
The world a canvas, painted bright,
Where every twist is pure delight.

A parade of critters, all in line,
With comical steps, they twist and twine.
As shadows flicker, mischief grows,
In this reverie, laughter flows.

So lose yourself in this jovial space,
Where every heart finds its happy place.
In light and whimsy, we all believe,
In this dreamland, we laugh and weave.

Fables of a Chirping Oasis

In a land where laughter flows,
Crickets play their merry shows.
Bees in hats buzz through the air,
Tickling petals without a care.

Squirrels wear their finest ties,
Chasing one another, oh so spry.
Butterflies dance in silly pairs,
As the sun shines, all joy declares.

The frogs croak rhymes, a joyful spree,
While turtles groove in harmony.
Every tree tells a funny tale,
Echoing with a giggly gale.

Through the bushes, whispers twirl,
A world where silly dreams unfurl.
Underneath the moon's soft glow,
Laughter lingers, sweet and slow.

The Spry Grove

In a grove where funny creatures peek,
Laughter dances, quick and sleek.
Foxes in socks and rabbits in shades,
Chasing shadows through curly glades.

The owls hoot jokes beneath the trees,
As ants on stilts parade with ease.
Wobbly walls of wiggling green,
A playground where joy reigns supreme.

The grasses giggle with a breeze,
And daisies chuckle as they tease.
Jumping around in a playful race,
With silly grins on every face.

In this grove of relentless cheer,
Every heart forgets its fear.
Where sprightly souls can always play,
Fun and laughter lead the way.

Bouncing Blossoms

Bouncing blooms all around me sway,
Winking petals in bright display.
Singing buds, with teasing flair,
Make the sunbeam dance in the air.

With each puffy cloud overhead,
Giggles sprout where laughter spreads.
Bees do the cha-cha on sweet thyme,
Tickling flowers, lost in rhyme.

The ladybugs chuckle, round and red,
As sneaky ants dance on their tread.
Blossoms bob and bounce in fun,
Beneath the roguish, warming sun.

In this patch of crazy glee,
Nature's humor runs wild and free.
Swirling colors, a vibrant spree,
In the land of laughs, it's plain to see.

The Whimsy Wood

Deep in the wood where the whimsy grows,
Mischievous laughter happily flows.
Trees wear hats, vines play peek-a-boo,
Every step brings a giggle anew.

The rabbits host a comedy show,
As shadows prance to and fro.
With jumping jacks, the frogs combine,
In a woodland dance that's simply divine.

A breezy breeze whispers jokes aloud,
As giggling leaves swirl in a crowd.
Gnomes crack smiles with their wise old tales,
Turning frowns into cheerful trails.

With every breath, joy intertwines,
In the whimsy wood, where the heart shines.
Creating memories of laughter's embrace,
In this magical, funny place.

Mirthful Minutes

In the forest, laughter blooms,
With critters dancing to funny tunes.
Squirrels wear hats, hold tiny dreams,
While whispers float like playful beams.

Bubbles pop from a toad's wide grin,
Chasing each other, they dance and spin.
A rabbit juggles acorns on its nose,
As funny stories in the breeze flows.

Under trees, the shadows play,
Tickling thoughts that bounce all day.
Every rustle holds a surprise,
With giggles that sparkle like sunshine skies.

Laughter lifts, the heart takes flight,
In a world where joy feels so right.
Moments frolic in a light-hearted race,
Happiness found in this enchanting place.

The Merry Clearing

In the clearing where fun convenes,
Colors burst where laughter gleams.
A raccoon with a rubber duck,
Splashing joy with a playful pluck.

Trees sway to the tickling breeze,
As whispers travel with such ease.
Crickets hold night concerts bright,
With notes of chuckles that dance with light.

A bear tells jokes with a jovial roar,
While butterflies flutter, begging for more.
Each flower giggles, their petals sway,
Sharing secrets of a sunny day.

Moonlight casts shadows, a delicate sight,
Painting the world in soft delight.
In this space, where spirits chase,
Laughter echoes, a warm embrace.

A Tickle in the Trees

Up in the branches, a squirrel prances,
With acorns rolling in joyful glances.
A parrot mimics a giggling sound,
As the wind plays tricks all around.

Frogs leap high, with a bellyache,
Telling tales that make us shake.
Each croak is a punchline, crisp and bright,
Filling the forest with pure delight.

The sun peeks through leaves, a warm embrace,
As shadows dance in a merry race.
The light-hearted buzz of bees on the wing,
Sings of joy and the fun they bring.

A tickle of laughter fills the air,
As the playful spirits frolic without care.
Where every creature finds their place,
In nature's funny, loving space.

Playful Reflections

In the pond, a mirror of glee,
Where frogs trade stories so carelessly.
Tadpoles wiggle with curious flair,
As ripples echo laughter in the air.

Wildflowers dance in a silly line,
Winking at the world, sparkling fine.
A chipmunk shares jokes with a grin,
As the world spins merrily, drawing us in.

The sky above, a canvas of dreams,
Paints chuckles with its sunny beams.
Every moment, a playful treasure,
Each laugh a note of pure pleasure.

In this realm where joy takes flight,
Worries fade into the soft twilight.
Here in the woods, mirth knows no end,
Nature's own laugh, our dear friend.

Jubilant Trails

In the woods where laughter streams,
Silly squirrels play in gleams.
Bouncing bunnies skip with glee,
Nature's joy is wild and free.

Ticklish winds tickle the trees,
Whispers of fun dance with ease.
Every turn brings a new surprise,
Smiles reflected in bright eyes.

Playful shadows leap and twirl,
In this enchanting, vibrant swirl.
Critters chuckle, echoes ring,
In the trails, joy's the king.

As the sun dips, colors fade,
Memories of fun will invade.
With every step, a laugh resounds,
On jubilant trails, joy abounds.

Secrets of the Merry Thicket

In a thicket where giggles bloom,
Frogs in bow ties paint the room.
Chickens wearing hats parade,
Life's a joke, all worries fade.

Dancing leaves, a cheeky ballet,
Hedgehogs burst into a play.
Whimsy weaves through branches high,
Silly secrets, oh my, oh my!

Elves sneak snacks behind the bark,
Giggling softly, leaving a mark.
Caterpillars don their shades,
In this merry thicket's glades.

Through the branches, laughter sings,
Joyful moments, a treasure brings.
In this thicket, nothing's bleak,
Embrace the funny, that's the peak.

Lively Shadows

In the twilight, shadows play,
Jumping high, they dance away.
Witty whispers float on air,
Lively spirits everywhere!

Bouncing beams of jade and gold,
Every corner holds a story told.
Mischief hides beneath the glow,
Where laughter flows, and mischief grows.

Twirling leaves in wild delight,
Silly shapes in the fading light.
Watch the moonbeam prance and sway,
In this lively, fun-filled way!

Just beyond the dappled trees,
Giggles linger in the breeze.
In shadows bright, our hearts take flight,
Embracing joy until the night.

The Humorous Clearing

In a clearing where laughter rings,
Jesters dance with playful flings.
A toad sings songs, oh what a sight,
Filling the air with sheer delight.

Bumblebees buzz in quirky tune,
Swaying 'neath the merry moon.
With each chuckle, hearts grow light,
In this humorous, happy night.

Witty rabbits spin their yarns,
Unicorns prancing on soft fawns.
Every giggle, a thread of cheer,
In a clearing where friends draw near.

As the stars begin to gleam,
Join the laughter, live the dream.
In this place where joy is clear,
Every moment, we hold dear.

Meadows of Mirth

In fields where laughter echoes clear,
A bumblebee buzzes, full of cheer.
Flowers dance in the warm sun's glow,
Tickling toes as they sway and flow.

With the wind, a tickling breeze,
Grass giggles softly, sways like tease.
A rabbit hops, a playful prank,
Flopping ears as he takes a prank.

Up in the sky, clouds float and grin,
Reflecting joy that's pure within.
Sunshine spills like golden wine,
Each beam a giggle, oh how divine!

When shadows stretch and whispers grow,
Even the crickets put on a show.
In meadows bright, where spirits twine,
The heart feels light; oh how we shine!

Treetop Serenades of Joy

High above, where branches sway,
A squirrel prances, bright and gay.
Leaves rustle softly, a giggling song,
Nature's laughter, where we belong.

A woodpecker taps in a rhythmic beat,
While chattering birds find a seat.
They chirp their secrets, weaving delight,
Serenading shadows, morning till night.

Swinging vines play twirls in air,
Inviting hearts with a playful dare.
Rays of the sun filter through the trees,
Whispering jokes on a gentle breeze.

A picnic spread beneath the green,
Boys and girls laughing, a happy scene.
In the canopy above, joy takes flight,
In the treetop realm, everything feels right!

Nature's Playful Chorus

Beneath the arch of the laughing sky,
Ants march in rhythm, oh my, oh my!
Each step a giggle, a jolly tune,
While daisies twirl to a sunlit rune.

Frogs puff their chests, croaking away,
Joining the chorus, come join and play!
The brook ripples softly, splashing around,
In every drop, a chuckle is found.

Butterflies flutter with a wink and a twirl,
Painting the air in a colorful swirl.
They flirt with the blooms, oh what a sight,
A spectacle merry, from morning till night.

In Nature's choir, the giggles arise,
With every note, under blue skies.
The world is a stage, where fun is the core,
In this playful chorus, we all want more!

Jests Beneath the Verdant Canopy

Under the leaves, where shadows prance,
A playful fox joins the frolic dance.
With a flick of his tail and a mischievous grin,
He teases the fawns, let the games begin!

A puddle reflects the sky's bright face,
Where splashes erupt, in this joyful space.
Each ripple a story, each laugh a spark,
In the heart of the woods, where spirits embark.

A chubby chipmunk hoards tasty treats,
While giggling children bounce on their feet.
Together they share their secret stash,
A treasure of smiles, oh what a splash!

As twilight creeps and stars spark above,
The night hums softly, wrapped in love.
Beneath this canopy, laughter takes flight,
With jests all around, through day and night!

The Frolic of Curious Creatures

Amidst the trees, the critters play,
Chasing shadows, bright and gay.
Squirrels leap with cheeky grins,
While hedgehogs twirl in soft, warm spins.

Bunnies bounce with wiggly tails,
Rabbits dance while the wind exhales.
Funny faces, wide-eyed surprise,
As laughter echoes under sunny skies.

A chipmunk slips on green, smooth grass,
Landing in a quirk—a funny pass.
They gather round, with glee and cheer,
Celebrating joy, it's all so clear.

In harmony, a merry band,
Each creature struts, the best they can.
With every giggle, every glance,
The forest bustles in a happy dance.

Hidden Hilarity in the Wild

In shadows deep where laughter hides,
The clever fox slips, with joyful strides.
A laugh escapes from leafy boughs,
As raccoons tumble like playful cows.

A surprising sight, two birds in flight,
Chasing their shadows in morning light.
With clumsy flaps, they swerve and dip,
Laughter boiling from every quip.

Beneath the ferns where secrets lay,
A gathering of friends, they come to play.
With whispers soft, sharing a jest,
In wild embraces, they feel so blessed.

Nature chuckles in vibrant hues,
Tickling petals of dancing dews.
In this wild world, filled to the brim,
The joy of life finds rhythm and whim.

Radiant Rays and Raucous Laughter

Sunlight filters through leafy seams,
A canvas brushed with playful dreams.
The merry sounds of nature sing,
In every corner, joy takes wing.

A turtle tumbles, slow but spry,
While frogs perform a leap and fly.
Silly songs of crickets sound,
As butterflies dance, twirling around.

The brook giggles with water's play,
Tickling stones along its way.
Chirping birds join in the fun,
Celebrating life beneath the sun.

With radiant beams and laughter bright,
The woods are filled with sheer delight.
Each moment bursts with joy anew,
In nature's realm, so vivid and true.

Jolly Journeys Through the Thicket

Through tangled trails where giggles flow,
    Adventures rise in charming show.
    With every turn, a surprise awaits,
As woodland folk laugh while fate navigates.

A rabbit hops with a springy cheer,
    Leading friends to fun so near.
    A dance of joy, a merry chase,
In this thicket, there's laughter's embrace.

Bushy tails and wiggly ears,
Filled with glee, there are no fears.
They scamper past the wildflowers bright,
    Collecting whispers of pure delight.

With every step in this jolly spree,
Life's humor shines, wild and free.
In the heart of the thicket, mischief beams,
Creating bonds through laughter's dreams.

Chortle Beneath the Canopy

Beneath the leafy laughter, bright,
A squirrel slips, oh what a sight!
The branches shake, the leaves they sway,
As giggles dance the day away.

In twilight's glow, the shadows play,
With whispers soft, they tease and sway.
A jolly frog hops here and there,
While fireflies twinkle in the air.

Nature's Whimsical Whispers

A breeze that tickles trees so tall,
The playful winds, they seem to call.
With hints of giggles in their flight,
They swirl around in pure delight.

The blossoms smile, their colors bright,
And butterflies join in the flight.
With every rustle, secrets shared,
In nature's joy, we're all ensnared.

Bliss in the Bundles of Bloom

Among the petals soft and sweet,
The merry bees begin to greet.
With buzzing laughs, they dance and spin,
A chorus born from deep within.

The daisies nod, the tulips sway,
As laughter spills from buds today.
In every hue, joy's song resounds,
In fragrant fields, pure bliss abounds.

Adventures in the Laughing Wood

In woods where silly sprites reside,
Each step we take, we're filled with pride.
For every knot and twisty trail,
A chuckle hides, a giggle's ale.

The birds proclaim with merry tunes,
While shadows play in bright balloons.
An acorn falls, a rabbit hops,
With antics known to make us stop.

The Joyful Understory

Beneath the leaves, a chuckle lay,
Where shadows dance and children play.
A tickling breeze, a whispering sigh,
Joyful secrets float and fly.

With flowers grinning, colors bright,
Every petal shares delight.
The playful critters hop around,
In this laughter-filled playground.

The sun peeks through, a warm embrace,
A silly squirrel darts with grace.
Mysteries hide behind each tree,
In the merriment, we feel so free.

And as we wander, giggles ring,
Nature's music starts to sing.
The understory, a mirthful place,
Where every face wears a smiling trace.

Chasing Sunbeams

Sunbeams chase the laughter wide,
Through fields where playful spirits hide.
We skip and jump, carefree and bold,
In this realm, where dreams unfold.

A butterfly winks, a trickster fair,
While daisies giggle without a care.
The clouds above form silly shapes,
As we create our wild escapes.

Listen close, the trees confide,
Stories of joy they cannot hide.
With every step, the world feels bright,
Chasing sunlight, pure delight.

Holding hands, we dance and sway,
In this place, we long to stay.
For every laugh, and every beam,
We're intertwined in a sunny dream.

Laughing Landmarks

The hills are rolling, giggles soar,
The paths we wander, tales galore.
Each landmark holds a secret shared,
In this funny world, we are bared.

A tree with branches like a jester,
Waves and laughs, our joyful tester.
The bubbling brook plays a tune,
As frogs join in, beneath the moon.

A rock that's shaped like a silly hat,
Invites us in, let's have a chat.
We sketch our dreams in branch and stone,
Here, laughter echoes as we roam.

With every step, the world feels bright,
Each laughing landmark ignites our light.
As we gather stories, old and new,
The joy of life shines right on through.

The Happy Haven

In a clearing where the wild things grin,
Laughter dances, spinning within.
With every breeze, a gentle tease,
Nature's joy puts minds at ease.

The rabbits play a joyful game,
While buzzing bees hum songs, the same.
A patch of daisies nods along,
In this happy haven, we belong.

The sun dips low, painting the sky,
With bursts of colors, oh my, oh my!
We twirl and laugh, our spirits light,
In this refuge, all feels right.

As twilight falls with a gentle sigh,
Stars peek out, shy as we try.
In this place, we pause and weave,
Stories of joy we now believe.

www.ingramcontent.com/pod-product-compliance
Lightning Source LLC
Chambersburg PA
CBHW051636160426
43209CB00004B/674